LUSTER OF JADE:

POETRY, PAINTING, AND MUSIC

Catherine Yi-yu Cho Woo

Seventh University Research Lecture
San Diego State University

Graduate Division and Research

San Diego State University Press

ISBN 1-879691-09-4 (cloth)

Published by
San Diego State University Press

San Diego State University
San Diego, CA 92182

Contents

The University Research Lecture Series

The University Research Lecture series recognizes San Diego State University faculty members for outstanding achievement in research and scholarship and fosters continuation of such accomplishments. Distinguished resident faculty scholars are able to share their knowledge more broadly with the academic community and the community at large through the presentation of all-university graduate colloquia on generic problems of research and graduate education. These colloquia combine open lectures of general interest with smaller seminars and workshops for the graduate students and faculty who are actively pursuing research in areas related to the colloquia topics. The series is sponsored by the Graduate Division and Research and the University Research Council and is supported in part through Instructionally Related Activities Funds. Each academic discipline or department which offers a graduate degree at San Diego State University may nominate resident faculty to participate in the series. Exposure to and interaction with such distinguished researchers is an integral part of the instructional experience for all graduate students at San Diego State University. Each of the lectures in the series will be published to assure their increased availability to the students and faculty of the university and to the community at large. This book, *Luster of Jade: Poetry, Painting, and Music*, originated as San Diego State University's Seventh University Research Lecture.

Dean Bartel:
Good morning. I'm Brad Bartel, Associate Dean of the Graduate Division, and on behalf of the Graduate Division and Research and the University Research Council, I'm delighted to welcome you today to this morning's colloquium with Professor Catherine Woo. As you know, this colloquium is one of a number of events scheduled in conjunction with the University Research Lecture, which Dr. Woo will deliver this afternoon at 4:00 p.m. in the Don Powell Theatre. Dr. Woo will be speaking on "The Luster of Jade: Poetry, Painting, and Music." This morning's colloquium provides an opportunity for faculty, graduate students, and guests from the community to interact with Dr. Woo on a somewhat more informal basis, though perhaps in a more technical way than would be possible at this afternoon's major lecture. At this point, I would like to turn over the proceedings to Dr. Charlotte Webb, Chair of the Department of Linguistics and Oriental Languages, who will introduce our honored speaker. Dr. Webb.

Dr. Webb:
I would like to welcome you again. It is nice to see all of you out there. I think this is a particularly appropriate time to have Dr. Catherine Woo as our honored guest because it helps us celebrate the Chinese New Year, just one more way that we can acknowledge the passing of this important time. Dr. Woo has been a professor at San Diego State since 1969, and the Chinese program started with Dr. Woo's presence on this campus. Due to her guidance, her knowledge, and her care, the Chinese program today is healthy and flourishing, and it is growing in very important ways. Dr. Woo is the Director of the Center for Asian Studies and also Director of the Chinese language program within our

department. She is an internationally known and recognized scholar in many different areas. She has published more than eight books and numerous articles. She has also written lyrics for many songs, one of these being the award-winning popular Chinese song, "Tian Tian Tian Lan." As well as being a well-known and respected scholar, she is also an exceptional artist, and she excels in this area just as she excels in the others that I have mentioned. Her paintings have been shown in China, Japan, and throughout the United States. Her art has been exhibited at Stanford University, Harvard University, and many other museums in Tokyo and, of course, throughout China. Currently, she is a commissioner here in San Diego for arts and culture for our city. I might say that one of her recent crowning honors, and certainly not her last, is that she recently was appointed by President Bush to be a member of the National Council on the Arts; she succeeds Marvin Hamlich. This is an honor, indeed. It's an honor for me and I am very happy to introduce to you our University Research Lecturer for 1991, Dr. Catherine Yi-yu ChoWoo.

Dr. Woo:
Good morning. I am so very happy to see so many of you. Some of you I have never seen before, such as the students studying Japanese who came with their teacher. But others are old friends of mine—some of my former students from ten, fifteen, twenty years ago, who now look so distinguished, coming in high heels and beautiful dresses, driving 120 miles from Los Angeles. I have friends who flew here from San Francisco. I have two of my mentors here today. I would like especially to introduce them in case you are busy and cannot come to the four o'clock "song and dance" presentation that I am going to do for you— Professor Lin Yun (林雲) and Professor Leo Chen (陳立鷗). I would like you to know that Professor Leo Chen is the professor who wrote the music for "Tian Tian Tian Lan," winner of the Golden Caldron Award. We were very fortunate. Our song became a popular hit in Taiwan and was the theme song for a nightly TV show for several seasons. We were very surprised, but we are very happy that we can share it with so many friends; we made many new friends because of "Tian, Tian, Tian Lan" (天天天藍).

Today, looking at the audience, I see friends that I know from Phi Beta Kappa. I see friends from the Center for Asian Studies. I see my dear Dean, who helped us to arrange student exchanges with Taiwan, Dr. Larry Feinberg. I will not make him stand up because he hurt his leg and came on crutches so we will just smile at him. I see Big John Cowart, who wrote a letter saying that he will always remember that when I was teaching I always said "Please, watch" whenever I went to the blackboard. So in a little while I will say "Please watch" when I demonstrate calligraphy for you.

There is one very important person whom I want to introduce because, although some of you have known me for twenty or thirty years, one person has known me longer than any of you, my mother. She is eighty-three years old, and she was an infant nurse for many years. I am very proud of her. I draw much of my energy from her.

Since I am going to be doing some calligraphy for you, I thought perhaps you would like to know how I got started as an artist. It was spring in Old Peking, and the willows were swaying with their new, tender green leaves. In a study lined with glass cases and shelves of old books at a large table, similar to this, an elderly gentleman was writing huge Chinese characters, each about three feet square. The room was so quiet that you could hear the brush kissing the paper. Several people were standing by watching. Among them was a three-year-old girl in the arms of her nurse. Patiently and silently she waited for *"Yeye"* (爺爺). The word for "Grandpa" in Chinese is *"Yeye."* My husband Peter and I have three grandchildren. Our daughter-in-law is Italian-American so our grandchildren speak English, but they know a few words of Chinese, and one of them is *"Yeye"* because *Yeye* always gives them candy. Do you know how to say grandpa in Chinese now? Whoever can say that will get candy in my office.

The three-year-old knew that when *Yeye* finished it would be her turn to "write." She would be allowed to finish all the ink left in *Yeye's* huge inkwell. Soon the floor was lined with several of *Yeye's* pieces of calligraphy. Smiling, he reached for the girl and said, "Yu, come." My name is Yu, which means "jade." That is why my talk today is entitled "Luster of Jade." I climbed on my grandfather's lap and learned how to hold a brush as a special treat. I was taught how to hold a brush, how to let the brush soak up ink from the inkwell—just the right amount. How many of you are taking the painting class from me? You are learning how to pick up ink, just the right amount. It takes practice.

As I grew older, I had the special privilege of pulling *Yeye's* paper when he wrote elongated copulas. Today, my student Susan Gehring will have that honor. Today, after fifty years, I can still hear *Yeye's* kind, loving voice saying, *"Kan zhe yeye xie* (看著爺々寫), "Pay attention to how grandpa writes." That's where I learned the phrase "Please, watch."

Calligraphy is considered to be one of the significant contributions of the Chinese artistic genius to the world of art. Now I shall demonstrate that art. But before I do that, I would like to very briefly explain what I am going to write. How many of you have heard of the ancient Chinese classic called the *Yi Jing* (易經)? [a show of hands from the audience] Very good. Some of you know it as the *Book of Changes*. It is one of the Five Classics that greatly influenced Chinese culture, Chinese thinking, and Chinese behavior.

Today, Professor Lin Yun [an expert on the *Yi Jing*] is here with us. I can't let him listen without doing something himself, right? I twisted his arm, and he agreed to give a talk tonight at seven o'clock. If you have time, I would like to personally invite you to attend. You will learn from him, because I have learned so much myself from Professor Lin, not only philosophy but literature as well. Once I was having an art show at the University of Massachusetts in Amherst, and Professor Lin had also been invited to give a lecture there. That night, at Professor Cheng Ching Mao's house there were several professors from Yale and Harvard, and we were doing calligraphy. We were all trying to memorize some ancient Chinese poems and write them out. Professor Lin was able to memorize more poems than those Chinese professors from Yale and Harvard.

In the *Yi Jing* there are eight trigrams and sixty-four hexagrams, and each one represents something. Today, I am going to write the character "*xun*" (巽) for you in this corner; it means "wealth." But if you look in the dictionary, it also can mean something that is going very smoothly. Oh, here is my other mentor, Professor John Tsu from the Department of Education. He is the Western Region Representative of the Secretary of Education and just flew in from San Francisco.

In the *Book of Changes* the character "*xun*" means "wind." In China we have a proverb, originally taken from a famous Chinese novel, *The Romance of Three Kingdoms*. It says "*wan shi ju bei zhi qian dung feng* (萬事俱備只欠東風)"—"The Ten Thousand Things are ready to go, only the East wind is missing." I am going to write this character so that you will receive the wind I am sending you. Whatever you are doing, if it is near completion, it is only lacking the final ingredient, the wind. Sometimes "the wind" may represent money. You may have completed your plans, and everything is all set, so you just need a little bit of something to finish it off. If you just get the money, then you can go forward.

Speaking about the Chinese New Year, here are the twelve animals. This year is the Year of the Ram, the next year will be the year of the Monkey, and then the Rooster, and then the Dog, and the Pig, and the Mouse, and the Cow . . . it always goes in the same order.

This is a piece of rice paper. Rice paper has a very different personality from watercolor paper. Have you all had rice? [The audience responds affirmatively.] This is not really made out of the rice that you eat, but this rice paper is very, very absorbent, like a thirsty person. It will soak up every drop of water that touches it. When you use rice paper, you have to use the proper amount of ink, the proper amount of pressure, and keep the brush on the paper the proper amount of time in order to get the desired result. My mentors,

Professor Lin and Professor Leo Chen, are all master calligraphers. In China we say, *"ban men nung fu"* (班 門 弄 斧   )— "an amateur trying to show off in front of masters." Please, forgive me, but this is part of my job as a University Research Lecturer today.

I will share a secret with those of you who paint. I am using two pieces of felt. This piece of felt will soak up the extra ink from the rice paper. If I do not use two pieces of felt when I use an especially huge brush like this, the ink will go through the paper onto the felt. If I pull the paper, the ink may be smeared. However, this way when I pull, the top piece of felt goes along with it so there is no danger that the ink will be smeared.

I was told this TV camera would show only this center area so I am going to write a huge character for you right now. Please, don't blink. If you blink, you might miss it. When I do a huge character, I always do it standing up. The strength is supposed to go from my heart to my shoulder, then through my arm to the tip of the brush and onto the paper. It is great fun doing huge characters because in one stroke you can get rid of all your frustrations. Traditionally, normally, I would use this inkstick and grind it on the ink stone. It takes about a half an hour to make enough ink to do a huge character. But today, I didn't think you wanted to watch me grind ink for half an hour so I compromised and used the liquid ink. I must ask forgiveness from my grandfather in heaven. This is not "kosher." It is not the authentic, traditional way. Normally, if you have time, you really should grind your ink. While you are grinding the ink, you acquire tranquility in your heart. Today, since I am with my masters, I already have tranquility in my heart so I don't need to grind the ink. Now, please watch. [Dr. Woo writes the two-foot square large character.]

Red is a happy color for the Chinese—it is used for weddings, for New Year, for childbirth, for birthdays. See how pretty Deborah looks in her red dress. She is dressed for the Chinese New Year. I am going to put a few red flowers on here for you. The flowers I am trying to do are plum flowers. The plum blossom is the national flower of China because a plum blossom is the first flower to bloom in the Spring. How many of our Chinese students in the back are from Taiwan? Do you know how to sing the song "Mei Hua?" Those of you who know how to sing it, let's sing "Mei Hua" while I'm painting " 梅花 ", the plum blossom. [Dr. Woo sings with the audience.] What we are saying is "Plum blossom, plum blossom, all under heaven." Then we talk about how, the colder it gets, the more it blooms. The plum blossom stands for courage, as our national flower symbolizes the courage of the Chinese people.

In the Western world when you do any piece of art work, you pay attention to balance. How many of you have been to Europe? Have you been to some of the beautiful gardens? Lucy Fleischman, which gardens have you been to? In those fancy gardens there are sculptures, there are cypress, there are fountains, but if you close one eye and look at only half of the garden often, when you see a sculpture here, there is likely to be a sculpture there. Many formal gardens are symmetrically balanced. How many of you have been to Japan or China? In our gardens, in our art, painting or calligraphy, we also aim at balancing the composition. However, often it is asymmetrical balance; nevertheless, it is balanced. I am showing you an example of asymmetry as I paint these flowers. I am trying to make it appear balanced on the sheet but not using symmetrical balance.

When I teach my students to paint, I sometimes tell them, "When you paint flowers, don't make all the flowers smile at you." Remember that some flowers should be smiling at you, and some flowers should be smiling at other people. If all the flowers are the same size and are smiling at you, like the sunflowers that follow the sun, the picture will appear unnatural. It would be prettier if you follow the papa bear, mama bear, baby bear theory—make some flowers big, some small, some full blown, some little buds, some smiling at her, some smiling at him.

Now I am finished with the brushwork, but I am not really done with the piece. Who can tell me what is missing? I signed! What's missing? Seals! Those of you who have been to a museum or have any kind of Chinese paintings or have even seen reproductions have seen the red seals on them. Often I am asked, "What are those?" They are seals. Sometimes they are the seals of the artist. When a calligrapher or a painter finishes their work, they will sign it and then they will add their name seal. Sometimes famous scholars who are curators are asked to judge the authenticity of a piece. If they say, "Ah, this is authentic," then they write a short paragraph, "I, so and so, looked at this. Yes, it is authentic." Then it carries a kind of "Good Housekeeping seal of approval." During the Ch'ing dynasty in particular, there were some Chinese emperors who especially loved art. When they saw a nice painting that they knew would be handed down for many, many generations, they wrote a little poem there and signed their names. Their names would go down in history. Sometimes collectors also put their seals on. That's why when you go to a museum to look at a piece of very famous art work, there may be many seals on it.

Talking about seals, do you know what color the ink usually is? Calligraphy often is done in black ink although sometimes it may be red. In the case of seals, an oil-based red ink is normally used. The only exception is when a person is in mourning for his or her parents. People come to pay their respects, and when thank you notes are written, blue ink is used. Otherwise, the ink is almost always red.

The seal can be made out of almost any material—bamboo, jade, stone, horn, ivory, wood, or even rubber. We divide the seals into two main types. In one type, *zhu wen* (朱文), the characters are shown in red. Everything is carved away except the character so that when you apply the ink you see the writing appear in red. The other kind is called *bai wen* (白文). In this type the characters appear in white because they are carved away while the rest of the seal is red. I will use both kinds so later on when you come up to look, see if you can distinguish the red characters from the white ones.

In addition to showing your name, the seal could bear your studio name [artist's pseudonym]. It could contain anything you like to say, reflecting your interest at that time. I have many seals. Of the many seals that I have, I brought a few samples to show you. In this little container I have five of them: one is round, one is square, and this one is rectangular. This is a fine piece of jade that I bought in Mainland China during one of my trips some years ago. The seal is the finishing touch on a piece of art work.

Let me tell you a simple technique to avoid putting your seal on upside down. If your seal has been carved by a famous carver or scholar, he will have his name or some statement inscribed on the left side. If you hold the seal with the writing facing your left, it will appear right side up. For those seals that don't have anything written on them, a mark can be made on the left side using a dab of red fingernail polish as a reminder to insure that you will not make a mistake.

This is a bamboo seal with my maiden name on it. I would like to share with you a Chinese tradition about names. If I attend some social function or party with my husband, Peter Woo, then I am known as Mrs. Woo. But as a professional, when I publish my books or have an art show or make recordings in China, all these are done under my maiden name, Cho Yi-yu (卓以玉). In China, working women use their maiden names professionally. People sometimes ask me, "Why is your name so long? Catherine Yi-yu Cho Woo. The computer cannot print all of it." I was born a Cho. My mom is Mrs. Cho. Yi is my generation name. All my cousins, brothers, everybody in my generation, bears the name Yi. Polly Liew over there went to college with one of my sisters, Cho Yi-ding (卓以定). When she heard my name was Cho Yi-yu, she said, "Oh, is Yi-ding one of your sisters?" The name "Catherine" I picked up while I was going to high school in Hong Kong. My mom named me after her best friend. Then I picked up the name "Woo" from Peter, my beloved husband.

Do you see the difference in the sizes of the seals? Professor Lin has some seals this big [indicating a six-inch square]. I am only his student so mine are only this big [indicating a four-inch square]. This one bears the name of my studio, *Ri Li Cao Tang* (日 文 艸堂), which means "thatched hut standing underneath the sun." This comes from a *mudra* about standing underneath the sun, trying to absorb the light and heat from the sun to benefit the body.

During the Tang Dynasty there was a very famous poet, Du Fu (杜甫). If you go to China and visit Chengdu (成都), I am certain the tour guide will take you to Du Fu's thatched hut, *Du Fu Can Tong* (杜甫草堂). Since I try to write poems, my master gave me this studio name *Ri Li Cao Tang*. I think he was hoping that I would be inspired by Du Fu to write some good poems.

I would very much like to present this to someone who has a large wall—Professor Charlotte Webb, for your new house. I hope everything goes very smoothly in our department, as well as in your private life. I would like to invite all of you to come up and look. If you would like to come up closer to look or to touch the seals or to look at what I have up here, you are welcome to do so. Since you have been sitting for a long time, I invite you to stand up and stretch your legs.

Dean Bartel:
We have some time for questions now, and if you would like to ask a question of Professor Woo, it would help us immensely if you would come to the microphone so that it could be recorded and then we can get some of the details of the calligraphy, its symbolism and history.

Dr. Woo:
A little while ago someone asked about the brush. This is a brand new brush made of bamboo, some kind of horn, and animal hair. It takes many years of training to make a fine brush like this. This is the same kind of brush after it has been used. I always tell my students when they first get a nice and trim brush that comes in a little holder, "That's like a teenager. Sweet sixteen, pretty and trim. After it has been used, it is like a slightly plump middle-aged lady." After it changes its shape, don't try to squeeze it into the sheath it came in. If you push this used brush into a very skinny little holder, you will ruin it. A good brush is not cheap, but its price is not necessarily related to its size. In the same way, even though some diamonds are bigger than this one [pointing to her ring], they are not as expensive as it is. Please remember, a penny is a penny's worth; you get what you pay for. If you buy a really poor brush, perhaps you will only be

able to draw some lines on ceramic pieces. You cannot really do detailed signs, calligraphy, or paintings. Also, it is very important to have the right equipment. The Chinese have a saying, "*gung yu shan qi shi bi xian li qi qi* (工 欲 善 其 事 必 先 利 其 器)—"You have to have the right tools because you cannot do brain surgery with a butcher's knife."

Brushes come in various sizes. We use the fine little ones to do fine work and the huge brushes to do large characters. After you use it, you should always rinse it and wash out the paint and color, whatever the foreign object is in the brush and then try to dry it. I always put my brushes in here [pointing to the bamboo mat] after I use them if I am going to carry them around. If I use this brush, it will still be wet after I rinse it. Even after I dry it on a paper towel, it is still damp. Please remember, the tip is made of hair and the handle is bamboo. How do they stay together? They are glued together, and often a water-soluble glue is used. If you leave your brush here in the water and go to watch TV, a football game, or CNN, or whatever, and forget about it for a few days, when you come back later, the tip might be divorced from the bamboo handle. All the king's men and all the king's horses cannot put it back together again. There goes your $30 brush. Always take good care of your brushes.

This bamboo mat brush holder is not a sushi maker, even though it looks like one. Once when I sent my students out to buy them, they bought some about two-thirds this length, and said, "Dr. Woo, it's very expensive." I said, "What did you get?" "We got a sushi maker." If you cannot find one of these brush holders, you can use a bamboo place mat. You can wrap the brushes in there, but this one is made for this purpose; it has a string to secure the brushes. If you don't have a string, you can still roll it to protect your brush because when the tip is wet, whatever form it dries in it is going to keep. If you stuff it in your backpack, you might have a brush that is twisted and crushed. Don't wrap it in plastic or saran wrap because the moisture will remain and it might dissolve the glue.

Dr. Carmichael:
Dr. Woo, I would like you to explain to us the significance of the orange on the table.

Dr. Woo:
A very good question, Nancy. I was going to talk for five minutes about the Chinese New Year. Since we mentioned the Chinese New Year, I thought it was very appropriate to explain it to you. This is an orange, but in Chinese it is called "*ji* (桔)." This sounds the same as, *ji* (吉), which means "good luck." For

Chinese New Year there are always many oranges or tangerines. If you visit any traditional Chinese family, they will have many oranges. We say "*ji xiang* (吉祥)." You try to let the good luck rub off on you so we always like to have oranges around. For Chinese New Year we have red envelopes like this. Usually there is some kind of lucky wish written on it in gold. This one says "*ru yi* (如意)," "everything as you wish." Isn't that nice? Professor Ray Smith, I hope in this new year of the Ram everything will happen as you wish.

In China, the Chinese New Year is the most important festival. It is like Thanksgiving, Christmas, and New Year all put together. Chinese families have a reunion. If the children are not working in the same city, they go home for New Year's. It is a time for family. If you go to China, and you can only spend three days in Taiwan or Hong Kong, don't go during New Year's because all the stores will be closed. The owners will be spending time with their families, and you will hear firecrackers all night long. Do you know why Chinese light firecrackers? Tradition says it is to ward off the evil spirits. This is just a Chinese folk belief. Now in Taiwan, some restaurants have a tape of firecracker sounds.

For Chinese New Year you may have seen the dragon dance. That is another thing Chinese do to celebrate. I want to explain for those of you who are not aware of why the Chinese love the dragon. The Chinese dragon is very different from western dragons. In the western world when you talk about dragons, you talk about beautiful maidens. The dragon spits fire and wants to eat the maiden, but then the knight comes on a white horse, kills the dragon, and saves the maiden. Then he marries her, and they live happily ever after. But China is traditionally an agricultural society so rain is very important. Even in twentieth century America we are concerned about the drought. We have to cut a certain percentage of our water use next month or pay a big bill. Chinese believed that the dragons live under the ocean in a crystal palace, and they are in charge of rain. They bring rain to the farmers. The farmers love the dragons because dragons represent water.

The emperors, knowing how the dragon represents power, put dragons on their robes. The emperors also have dragons on their bowls. Have you seen them in the museum? Other people like to have dragons as well. There is a dragon on my inkwell. A very clever person solved the conflict. The emperors have five-clawed dragons; the high officials have four-clawed dragons, and you and I have three-clawed dragons.

For the Chinese New Year we always serve a lot of sweet things because *tian* (甜), "sweet," is a pun for the character *tian* (添), "to add on." You add more money or more children. In America most people don't dare to have more than two children because you don't have any maids to take care of them. But traditionally in ancient China, especially on the farm in the countryside, the more children you have, the more sons you have, the more hands there are to work for the family. Also, the Chinese wanted to have sons to carry on the family name. The Chinese liked to have many children. They serve *lian zi* (蓮 子), lotus seed, because *lian zi* (蓮 子) sounds like *lian zi* (連 子), "continuously," that is, to continuously have children. That would scare some of you.

David Rosen:
You explained to us thoroughly regarding the different chops. The biggest one, of course, is your studio chop. You explained to us also regarding half a dozen chops. But I am puzzled as to why, on that beautiful rice paper, you have several small chops. Could you kindly explain to me the significance of each small chop?

Dr. Woo:
This one, a medium-sized chop, says "*shang le ni yin* (上 了 你 癮)"— " I'm addicted to you." That is the title of one of my poems and also the title of a song and an album that you can see on display in the library. I invite you to look at some of my other things in Love Library. There are paintings and pieces of jewelry and ceramics and sculptures, as well as books and articles. This chop, next to the bamboo chop, says Yi-yu (以 玉); "Yi" is my generation name and "*yu*," "jade," is my personal name. At the other end it says Cho (卓), my maiden name, my father's name. This little one says "*huei xin* (會 心)," you can translate it as "we think alike, we're good friends and buddies." These kinds of friends always bail me out whenever I need help. When we look at each other, we smile. We understand each other. We don't even have to say anything. Some of you are buddies, couples like Marty and Lucy Fleischman. You know each other so well. Before Lucy says something, Marty already knows what it is. If you go somewhere and you look at a beautiful sunset, Lucy doesn't have to tell Marty, "Look at that beautiful sunset." She just pokes him in the elbow, and they look at it and smile at each other. No explanation is needed.

Here is another seal; again it has my name, Cho Yi-yu, surrounded by four animals. This is a very unique seal. Some of you who study Chinese philosophy may know about the traditional meaning of the four animals, representing the four directions: *qing lung* (青 龍), the blue dragon, is on the east side; *zhu que* (朱 雀), the red phoenix, is the red bird on the south side; *bai hu* (白虎), the white tiger, is on the west side; and *xun guei* (玄龜), the turtle with the head of a snake in a dark color, is on the north side. This is the traditional concept of the heavens, the sky.

Over here is a little seal that says *wen chang ge* (文昌閣). Supposedly that is the constellation in charge of scholarship and brains. I need a lot of that since I am still trying to study and learn, and I hope to do well. I have a seal that says "*wen chang ge* (文昌閣)." Those are all the seals. Any other questions?

Dean Bartel:
Unfortunately, Catherine, I don't think we have any time for any more questions. I do want to thank you all for coming and being with us today at Professor Woo's colloquium. It was absolutely marvelous, and I want to invite all of you to come this afternoon at four o'clock to the Don Powell Theatre for the major public lecture. I think you'll be in for many very interesting surprises and an enjoyable time. Again, I would like to thank Professor Woo for her colloquium today. Thank you.

Dr. Woo:
Thank you for the honor. I especially would like to thank my Phi Beta Kappa friend Anne-Charlotte. She was on the committee that arranged for my being here today. Without their support I wouldn't be here today. Thank you.

President Day:
I am delighted to welcome you to San Diego State University's Seventh University Research Lecture. The University Research Lecture Series is a project sponsored by the Graduate Division and Research under the auspices of the University Research Council and supported by instructionally-related activities funds. The series was developed to honor annually resident faculty scholars for outstanding achievement in research and scholarship. Award recipients who are designated University Research Lecturer for the academic year deliver a general public lecture and engage in a variety of academic activities throughout the year designed to share their research more broadly with the academic community and the community at large. Each academic discipline or department has an opportunity to nominate a faculty member for this award. A faculty committee with representatives from each of the seven colleges makes the final recommendations to the Dean of the Graduate Division and Research, who selects the individual on behalf of the Research Council.

Today, Catherine Woo, Professor of Chinese in the Linguistics and Oriental Languages Department as well as an internationally known artist, poet, and composer, will present the Seventh University Research Lecture. I am confident that the University Research Lecture honoring our own faculty will continue to be an important part of our academic tradition. Right now I would like to present Dr. James Cobble, Dean of the Graduate Division and Research, who will introduce our honored speaker.

Dean Cobble:
Thank you, President Day. It is my honor to introduce Professor Catherine Woo, who was born Cho Yi-yu on May 23, 1934, in Beijing, China, into a

scholarly family. All four of her great grandfathers had received the highest of scholar degrees, *jin-shi* (進士) given in China. Her maternal grandfather had received an engineering degree at Cornell, and her father had attended graduate school at Columbia University. As an aside, I should note that the house in which Catherine was born had over one hundred rooms and once belonged to a Chinese princess. What a wonderful beginning to develop one's interest in the cultural arts!

After World War II, China was in the turmoil of a revolution. In 1949 Catherine left Shanghai for Hong Kong where she finished high school. Her family was interested in furthering her education abroad so Catherine came to the United States and enrolled in the School of Architecture at the University of Illinois. She remembers her introduction to life on her own and in a new country as a rude awakening and quite a culture shock in itself. For example, many of us have had the usual experience around the time we had to do our own laundry. Well, considering that most of Catherine's clothing was made of lovely Chinese silk, her first encounter with a dormitory washing machine was nothing less than horrifying.

One year before her architectural studies were completed at the university, she married an architect, Peter Woo, and moved to San Diego. For ten years she stayed at home to raise and educate her two children, Paul and Cindy. As the children spent more time in school, she began to take courses at San Diego State, first toward a bachelor's degree in interior design, then a master's degree in art history. While teaching Chinese full-time, she hitched a ride with the University of California library book van and traveled back and forth to UCLA working on a doctorate. She completed that work at the University of San Francisco with a dissertation on Chinese aesthetics. Between 1982 and 1988, scholar Woo simultaneously taught full time at San Diego State and part-time at San Francisco State, flying back and forth in what can only be surmised as her impractical love of and devotion to teaching. It is no wonder that Catherine credits her husband, Peter, with an amazing amount of understanding and support.

Dr. Woo is currently Professor of Chinese at San Diego State University in what has been a mutual love affair between the institution and this remarkable woman. It is impossible to summarize in this brief introduction the scope of her interest and talent. All things of beauty and creativity touching Chinese culture would, in itself, be an imperfect description. A perusal of some of the titles of some of her writings is an incredible experience. For example, one such title, "A Thousand Year Pine for All the Tender Hearts Under Heaven," partially demonstrates what I am trying to convey to you about her.

Author Woo will do a much better job in just a few moments.

Catherine is also a prolific artist. She has graced our campus, as well as the galleries at Stanford University, the Arthur M. Sackler Museum at Harvard University, and the National Gallery in Taipei, with lovely silk and brush paintings. Composer Woo has written lyrics for a number of award-winning popular Chinese songs, and her talent has contributed to an understanding of Chinese philosophy and aesthetics. Recognizing her international nature, the President of the United States a few days ago nominated Dr. Woo to membership on the National Council on the Arts, the advisory board that oversees the National Endowment for the Arts. If she lends her talent to that challenging position with the same enthusiasm she brings to all her other endeavors, I can only say, "Watch out, Washington!"

Professor Woo, Catherine, you have devoted a lifetime of study and scholarship to distinguished creativity which has enriched the lives of students and colleagues and thousands of citizens and friends of the cultural arts. In doing so, you have epitomized the highest calling for the university, one that the university community holds so dear. Mr. President, honored guests, members of the faculty, students, and friends of the university, it is my great pleasure to present to you the 1990-91 University Research Lecturer and one of the faculty's most distinguished scholars, Dr. Catherine Woo.

Dr. Woo:

I was born in China. In China we respect age. In China we respect our teachers. Today, as I am standing here feeling very, very honored, I want to honor my teachers. I saw Dr. Jansen sitting in the back. I took Political Science from him, and I would like to show you how Chinese really pay respect to their teachers. I have nine mentors. Right now I would like to invite six of my mentors who are alive to come on stage. Allan, Dr. Allan Anderson, my "Half-fairy Underneath the Moon," will you please come on stage? Ted, Dr. Ted Warren— I often say Ted is better than God. When we ask God questions, sometimes we don't get answers. Ted always gives me a very sensible answer. Dr. H. H. Chow (周鴻翔) from UCLA, where I finished my graduate work toward my Ph.D. degree in Chinese Language and Literature. Dr. John Tsu (祖炳民) helped me obtain a federal fellowship to write my doctoral dissertation at the University of San Francisco. Dr. Leo Chen (陳立鷗), a professor from San Francisco State University. Professor Lin Yun (林雲). [The six called mount the podium.]

As you see, there are three empty seats. I am sure there are three angels smiling up there. The first one is my grandfather, Professor T. M. Cho

(卓君庸). My grandfather started me as an artist by teaching me how to hold a brush to do Chinese calligraphy. The second seat is for my father, Professor Edward-Lai Cho (卓宜来). My father started me memorizing the Chinese classics when I was three or four. The seat between Professor John Tsu and Professor Leo Chen belongs to a very dear friend of Professor John Tsu and Professor Leo Chen, Professor Kai-yu Hsu (許芥昱), whose influence was invaluable. He encouraged me to write and paint. If you like my paintings, I would like you to know that he arranged for some of my first art shows. Professor Leo Chen composed the music of "Tian, Tian, Tian Lan" that you will hear later today, our number one hit. Professor Lin, Professor of philosophy, literature, and culture, has taught language. I have learned much from him, not only literature, art, and calligraphy, but how to behave, how to treat other people. Right now I want to show you how Chinese, since ancient times, have paid respect to their teachers. [Dr. Woo kowtows to all of the six seated on the stage, after which they file off the stage.]

So many times I have been asked, "Cathy, how can you do so many things? Where did you get the energy to do all these things?" Today, since the University is honoring me on this stage, I will share my secret with you. [Dr. Woo invites her family members to join her on the stage and introduces each of them in turn.] My mother is eighty-three years old. My husband Peter Woo (胡百昌)—I wish to thank him for not locking me in the "Doll's House." This is one of our three grandchildren, Elisabeth (胡晏洺). Our number-one grandson, Peter Kai-ray (胡啓瑞), is in school so he cannot be here. Our daughter-in-law, Mary, is with David (胡啓瑋), the youngest grandchild, who is too young to join us today. This is our number-one son, Paul (胡培為), who works for Apple computers. This is the best part of me, our daughter, Cindy (胡欣儀). She is doing post-doctoral research at UC Irvine in Psychobiology. Dear friends, this is my own private generator. I go home and recharge my batteries whenever I am with them. This is where I get the energy to do my work. [They return to their seats in the audience.]

Before I do my "show," I need to thank President Day, Vice President Al Johnson, Dean James Cobble, Associate Dean Brad Bartel, and a very, very special person, Deborah Janov. She has worked so hard, made so many telephone calls. She is one of those unsung heroines. Without her patience and perseverance, and working and working and working and smiling at different people, we could not have what we have today. I wish to thank Deborah. I wish to thank my friend, Professor Craig Wolf of the Drama Department. He is now in Boston attending a conference, but he was here last weekend hanging the lights, hanging the banners, and Monday he was here all afternoon setting up all the lights. I wish to thank Bill Hektner from the Drama Department for the audio and technical assistance; Rudy Vaca and Bill Behrens of Media Technology for video/audio assistance, and David Poddig. At first there was a big screen, but one-third of the room could see only one-third of the screen, and David helped me fix it and change the projector so I think later on most of you will be able to see.

I wish to thank Lin Zhong (林忠) and Shu Ling (淑珍), two beautiful Chinese students in telecommunications, who will be helping me show the slides and play the music. I wish to thank Dr. Janet Bedford and Dr. Richard Gerrero in Media Technology Services; Dean Paul Strand and Associate Dean Pat Huckle for all their help. I also wish to thank Jean Isaacs' 3's Company for sending six of their best dancers to do three duets for you. I wish to thank Professor Zhou Chia-sheng (周家聲) from Beijing. He will end our show with a piano piece that I wrote not too long ago, playing on the baby grand piano at the other end of the stage. The first dance is choreographed by Terry Wilson and will be danced by Eric Geiger and Odile Reine-Adelaide. Dance two is choreographed and danced by Kim Chidley and Faith Jensen-Ismay. Dance three is choreographed and danced by William Spencer Noble and Gail Olson. Now, shall we shart?

These two characters are *ju yi* (如意), which means everything will go as you wish (see figure 1). This is my wish for you, my dear friends. The Chinese New Year was only a few days ago so I can still wish you a happy Chinese New Year. May I wish that during this Year of the Ram everything will go as you wish.

This is a calligraphy painting done by Professor Lin Yun for my mother's eightieth birthday (see figure 2). In Chinese it reads *"fu ju dung hai chang liu shui; shou bi nan shan bu lao song* (福如東海長流水寿 比南山不老松)." It is a very special longevity wish so may I also share it with you and your loved ones and your elders.

This is an ink drawing that I did of Professor Lin Yun, who is here in the audience and who was on stage earlier (see figure 3).

THOUSAND YEAR PINE

Many grow quickly
          Like the mushrooms
One grows slowly
          Like an old pine
Summer sun
       Winter snow
            Summer sun
                  Winter snow
Withered the mushrooms
            Tested the pine.

I often tell my students, "I would rather you grow slowly but solidly like the old pine than grow very quickly like a mushroom and wither under the first snow"(see figure 4, "Pines").

BRUISES

I watch
      Clear brooks
           Dashing
              Downhill

And marvel at
      The beauty of
           Splashing
              White

Bruises
      From
          Hitting
            Rocks
              Unseen

Have many of you gone camping before? [Positive response from the audience.] Have you seen beautiful little brooks dashing down the hill hit a rock so you see the beautiful white splash? (see figure 5, "Misty Peak") Water does not bruise, but humans do. So often we only see the accomplishments of others. Little do we know of the midnight oil that has been burned and the sacrifices that were made.

SPLIT PEA SOUP

Split pea soup
　　　　One small can
　　　　　　My love shared with me

So rapidly
　　　　We drank
　　　　　　Smiling
　　　　　　　　Holding hands
　　　　　　　　　　From a
　　　　　　　　　　　　cracked
　　　　　　　　　　　　　　bowl

Before it leaked away. . . . .

[see figure 6, "Spring Greetings"]

Please note, this is not a five-clawed dragon bowl. It is not delicious shark fin soup. It is a very simple split pea soup, and yet, if you share it with someone you love, even in a cracked bowl, you are very happy.

WATER AND CLAY

Woman is
> Water
>> Man
>>> Clay.

Says
> One
>> Ancient
>>> Chinese tale

Potters
> Learn from
>> Potter's wheels

Without water
> Clay
>> Will not shape

Too much water
> Clay
>> Becomes
>>> Slip

I don't know if you have worked with clay before. Slip is that gooey, soft clay that you must discard. I'm sure you have seen in the newspaper famous politicians and ministers whose careers were ruined by too much water. (see figure 7, "A Patch of Bright Cloud").

SUN MOON LAKE

Green mountains
        Old pine
               Temple bells ring

Blue lake
        Young grass
               Field crickets sing

Serene
        Clouds move mountains
               Rain dimples lake

If you ever visit Taiwan, Republic of China, please reserve at least a few days for Sun Moon Lake (see figure 8, "Contemplating"). It is my favorite mountain lake. In the morning around five o'clock you can hear the bell from the temple across the lake. Dong, dong. There is mist hovering above the lake, and there will be clouds covering perhaps this mountain while you can see that mountain. In a little while, the cloud moves over and covers this mountain, and that mountain appears, as if the clouds have moved the mountain. Of course, the cloud cannot really move mountains. On summer days the rain just pours down, making hundreds and thousands of dimples on the face of that peaceful lake. I almost didn't come back!

WATERFALL

A
  Waterfall
      Clings
          All day
              To my rock

Shirt of
      Tender
          Velvety
              Moss

Singing
      Skipping
          Worldly worries
              Outward
                  Toss

[see figures 9 and 10 (close-up), "Quiet Roar"]

CONTEMPLATING

Contemplating
      Grand old mountains
          And
              Long hills

Broadens
      Your chest
          Furthers
        Your view

[see figure 11, "Immersed in Infinite Joy"]

My family and I love to go camping. Since our children Paul and Cindy were in diapers and drinking bottles, we went camping. When you look at those mountains which were there a thousand years ago and will be there two thousand years from now, you feel very minute. You feel very humble. Yes, we play a part in Nature but a very small part.

PEACOCK FEATHERS BLUE AND GREEN

Peacock feathers
　　　　Blue and green

Brought back
　　　　Young dreams on the screen

Near Forbidden City
　　　　In Central Park

Where Chinese children
　　　　Lingered till dark.

Peacock
　　　Peacock
　　　　　Do you know
　　　　　　Do my old friends' feathers
　　　　　　　　Still glow?

[see figure 12, "First Love"]

["First Love"]

This was a popular song in Taiwan. I will play and sing it for you while the dancers dance (see figure 13, Eric Geiger and Odile Reine-Adelaide). A very loose translation is:

Full moon in heaven;

On earth two young people fated to be together.

Holding hands, chatting, laughing

Treading on the echo of the pebblestone path walking toward her home.

Frantically beating, he took the heart that had leapt into his throat

And offered it to her. [their first kiss]

Two patches of pink clouds spread across her cheeks

Forever stored in the depths of his heart.

Whenever he is alone under the full moon

Those two patches of pink clouds softly pluck the strings of his heart,

Emitting strand after strand of intoxicating melodies

Taking him back to so many years ago,

Taking him back to so many years ago, so many years ago.

CHANGE

Hardship of life
        Left trails on
                Her once
                        Beautiful face

Pains of sorrow
        Ivoried
                Her once
                        Ebony hair

Tears of dolor
        Washed away
                Her once
                        Warm and
                                friendly smile

Scabs of scars
        Hardened
                Her once
                        Tender heart

Now
        People wonder
                If she is feelingless
        People wonder
                If she ever
                        Smiles or
                                Cries.

People wonder. . . . .

I often tell my students, if you see some grouchy old man or grouchy old lady, please be kind to them. Maybe they are experiencing excruciating pain.

[see figure 14, "Chance Encounter"]

CLOUDBURST

Mountain
>Mountain
>>Far and near

Cloud
>Cloud
>>Here and there

Mountains cold
>Clouds warm
>>Pour down rain

Hundreds
>Millions
>>Pearls
>>>Come home again

MT. WHITNEY HIKE

Lines of winter
>Marked
>>Grey face of Whitney

Halfway
>To
>>Heaven
>>>Whole soul
>>>>Enlightened

[see figure 15, "The First Glimpse of Afterglow"]

STRENGTH AND FLEXIBILITY

Water
>With
>>Strength and
>>>Flexibility

Gradually
>Cut through
>>Grand
>>>Old
>>>>Rocks

Pressed at dam
>Strength accumulated
>>>Volume
>>>increased

Limitations
>Overly imposed
>>Brought
>>>Breakdown

>Disaster
>>Chooses
>>No path

[see figure 16, "The Seas Frontage"]

SHAPE UP

She spoke harshly
          She hurt my pride

Looking deeply
          Into her eyes
                    I realized

Were there no
          Deep love
                    Trust and
                              Concern

There would be no
          Disappointment.

Shape up!
          I must!
                    Before I fade into
                              Nothingness

[see figure 17, "Contentment"]

MEMORIES

Memories
    Old
        Faded
            Yellow
                Memories
A smile
    A touch
        A whisper
            Of
                Yesteryear
                    Faraway

In the background
        Yet never gone
They were thrown away
        Yet they stayed
They are ours

[see figure 18, "Softly the Birds Sing"]

SORROW

Temple bells
        Winged angels
                Veiled head vigil

Flickering flame
        Dripping tears
                Yellowing glow

A single candle
        Lighted
            For you

VIOLET WISTERIA

LEANING
    CLIMBING
        TWINING
            Aged vine
                Picturesque trunk
Cluster of violent clouds
        Spring blossoms
            Splendid
                Divine

Translucent leaflets
        Filtering summer shades
Pendants of white jade
        Legumes swinging in autumn winds

Trellises'
    Harshness, softened

    As
        Winter sun
            Graces
                Leafless canes

Ah...
    Wisteria dear
        Trunk
            Muscular
              Hardy

Yet. . .Never
    Can stand FREE as a subtle slender bamboo!

("Missing You")

("Missing You")

[see figure 19, Kim Chidley and Faith Jensen-Ismay]

This is the music I wrote to accompany a poem by Dr. Kai-yu Hsu. (Dr. Woo sings with the taped music while the dancers dance.) Thank you, Kim, and thank you, Faith. That was beautiful.

[see figure 20, "Missing You"]

ROCKS

Others
    Fished
        Fish
           While I
               Fished
                  Rocks

They ate
    Fried fish
        As I watched

Tomorrow
    Their fish
        Will turn to
           White bones

But my rock
    Remain always
        White stones

[see figure 21, "Quivering Blue"]

SO MINUTE

In huge lake
      Floating
            On raft of
                  Fallen leaves

Surrounded by
          Snow capped
              Peaks

Among nature's majestic view
          The part
              I'm playing
                    so minute

[see figure 22, "Reverberating Blue"]

DON'T REALLY MIND IF I NEVER WAKE

Bed of
      Pine needles

Quilt of
      Moonlight
          Heavenly tent of stars

Rapids
      Singing
          Lullaby
With loved one
      Only
          A thought away

Don't really mind
      If
        I never wake.

[see figure 23, "Lush"]

Often when we go camping, I will try to write something. Sometimes everybody is asleep. One time in the dark I tried to scribble out some sentences that I really liked, and the next morning I looked. Only the first three words were there because I was writing upward. With a ballpoint pen you cannot write upwards. Now I have a felt-tip pen next to my bed.

GENTLY WATER RUBBED BACK OF ROCKS

Twilight fishing in
                    Mission Bay
Cast my line and
                    Frowns away

Seagulls
          Sailboats
                    Distant lights
                              Alone I sat many nights

To the wrinkled faced
                    Mother sea
I opened my chest
                    For her to see
She listened patiently
                    But did not talk
Gently water rubbed
                    Back of rocks

[see figure 24, "Neptune's Heraldry"]

Since Paul and Cindy were little, we often spent weekends fishing on Mission Bay. Those of you who fish will know that, even though you go with somebody, you sit alone to fish because if you sit too close, your lines will get tangled.

I LOVE

In the way of water
          I love
Things all luminous
              With magical sheen

He
    Accepted
         Forgiven
             Only love can

Onward
      Flow
         My tears

Quietly
      Gently
         I love

[see figure 25, "Temptation of Strength"]

RAIN

Gray is heaven
        Grayer the earth
The silk of rain weave together
                Heaven and earth
Countless rain pearls
        Adorning the trees
Each pearl concealing
        A youthful vision
The feelingless street light
                Coldly starting
At the earth nourished
        By broken dreams. . .

[see figure 26, "Bewitched by Spring Dream"]

I often tell my friends and students, God is very fair. Sometimes our dreams will come true. Sometimes they may not come true because it is someone else's turn to have their dreams come true. If you know that your broken dream is nourishing someone else's dream, maybe you can accept that broken dream a little bit better.

TO DAD

When you are gone
    There are so many words I have not yet said
It is like the leftover tea in the teacup
    After the guest has departed
The chance to chat
    The chance to sip
        Have both been missed
Casting my eyes westward
    There are still a few
        Lingering sunsets at dusk

When you are gone
    There are so many words I have not yet said
It is like after the clock strikes
    Time is hanging for one moment
        In mid-air
Can you hear it?
    Can you still hear it?
Casting my eyes westward
    There is a wheel, the full moon
        There are no stars

\When you are gone
    There are so many words I have not yet said
It is like the flute you always played under the full moon
    The music now
        Muted by silence
Carefully, I put away your flute
    But how can I put away my thought of you?
Casting my eyes westward
    Ai - inlaid in the dark of night
        Are stars
           Many stars.

Now you are gone
    There are so many words I have not yet said
And never will say
    I silently pledge
Tomorrow I'll learn to play your flute
    And practice what you've said
Casting my eyes westward
    The stars are low
        Against the pale white
            There flew the first bird
            Of the morning

[see figures 27, "Ch'i," and 28, "Plum Blossom Fragrance"]

("Tian Tian Tian Lan")

TIAN TIAN TIAN LAN [see figure 29 In Chinese]

This is our number one hit. It was the theme song to a nightly TV show in Taiwan for a long time and won quite a few awards. I wrote the first few lines of the poem. When my Uncle Leo put it to music, he said, "It's too short," so he added the last twelve words. I will loosely translate it for you.

Day after day after day, blue is the sky
Not to miss him, how could I?
The innocent child still asks,
"Why are your eyes perspiring?"
Deep is the affection, intense the feeling.
Parting is sorrowful, missing also empty.

[see figure 30, "Ch'i Soaring"]

I would like to dedicate this song today to my very, very dear and special friend Susan Coumatos, Manager of the Faculty-Staff Centre, whose husband is far away in the Persian Gulf. I know some of you have been to the library looking at my exhibitions of jewelry and songs and articles and books. You may have noticed that I sprinkled sand through all the shelves. Every little grain of sand is a special blessing for our troops in the Gulf. (Dr. Woo sings with taped music while the dancers dance.) [see figure 31, William Spencer Noble and Gail Olson]

And now to conclude the program, Professor Zhou Chia-sheng will play "Plum Blossom Fragrance," a song that I wrote both the lyrics and music to.

("Plum Blossom Fragrance")

Thank you. I would like to call on some very dear people that helped me put this together. Deborah Janov—she alone worked harder than all of us put together. I would like to have Lin Chung and Shu Ling and all the ushers please come up here. You sacrificed your afternoon on such a beautiful day. I would like to thank the students who are here to help me. Chu Ling was in charge of helping with the music, and may I please have the dancers come out.

Last but not least, I wish to thank all of you for spending the afternoon with us. Thank you, Dr. Susan Tsu; you came all the way here from San Francisco. Thank you, May Hsu, for driving to San Diego from Orange County with Dr. Chou.

Thank you, March Fong Eu, California's Secretary of State, my very special friend. March, would you please come up for a second? I have a lot of respect for March. One time I had an art show in her office in Sacramento. After the reception March and I flew back from Sacramento to Los Angeles together. During the one-hour flight she pulled out her Chinese book from her big purse, and we had one Chinese lesson on the plane. After looking at March, you will understand why they say, "I love Eu."

Thank you, Uncle Drum; thank you, Aunt Florence, my number-one American uncle, former U.S. ambassador to the Republic of China, Everett Drumright, and number-one American aunt. Thank you, Louise, my big sister. When we first came to San Diego in 1957, we were young and didn't know much. Louise and Daniel Chu loved us and took care of us, my big sister and big brother. I will always have a special place in my heart for them. Thank you, so many of you, I cannot name you all. Molly Lee, who helped me entertain my guests last night—even though you are so busy, you took time to come. Roxana Ou (江樂舜), former Miss China. Do you want to see what a Miss China looks like? Now she is a banker. Rong-rong Liew (金蓉蓉), my dear Rong-rong. She's very fortunate because she is very talented, and she has a beautiful house and is very generous. She always shares what she has. My cousin went to college with her, and I was told even then she shared with all her friends special candy that she received from her parents. I was happy to see Jan Domnitz; I was so happy to see Deborah Berren coming from Pepperdine University, and now she is a director of program administration. I'm happy to see Professor Arthur Springer. So many moons ago you were auditing Chinese. I cannot finish naming all my dear friends here. I just named a few, but I want everyone of you to know, I really appreciate you coming here to share this beautiful afternoon with me. I will remember this for a long, long time. Thank you.

March Fong Eu: (余江月桂)

Thank you very much, Cathy, for the opportunity to just say a few words to your many friends here. I feel very honored to have been invited to participate in this afternoon of celebration where we have been sharing the beautiful work of Dr. Catherine Woo. I think I join with all of you as we say to her, we thank her for this rich experience that she has given to us. Not just this afternoon, but what she gives us all the time. Thank you, Cathy, for all that you do for all of us in the work you do here in San Diego and for the world. Thank you, Cathy.

Yes, my friendship with Cathy goes back a good many years. That one lesson in Chinese didn't do me that much good, though. We have to ride the airplane more often together, Cathy, so I can finish up my course work. But I have had a great deal of inspiration watching Cathy over the years, and that one brief experience in trying to master five thousand years of Chinese in one hour was very rewarding because it has gotten me started in telling myself that, as an American-born Chinese and third-generation American, there was a lot of culture that I was lacking, so she did really give me a great deal of inspiration during that one hour. She doesn't know how much inspiration she gave me because not only did I have this fascination with the language, but now I've started just very recently, Cathy, you don't know about it, but I started trying to learn brush painting and calligraphy, and I thank you for all the inspiration that you've provided me. That's why when I came up here I said I think I should just stand up here with the rest of your students.

But I would like to put on my other hat this afternoon and present to you—because I think that this is such a very memorable experience and a memorable occasion—I'd like to give to you a proclamation from the State of California to remember this very important day of your life and our lives, and I hope that you will accept it from me with the good wishes of all the people of California, all of your friends, and the government of California.

Dr. Woo:
Thank you, March. Who else do I need to thank? Al Branan, without his impetus we wouldn't have a Chinese minor. Thank you, Al. I hope you channel more international business students to Chinese and Japanese. Thank you, Miki, thanks to so many of you. I hope you will go to the library and enjoy my display. Thank you, Helena, my dear, dear Helena.

President Day:
Thank you, Dr. Woo. It's my task to bring this happy occasion to a close. I told you the university is a remarkable place, full of remarkable scholars. You've seen one of our best, and with that kind of support, you can imagine the joy and spirit the university shares when those kinds of scholars are available to our students. Thank you all for coming, and we'll bring this occasion to a close.

3   *PUBLICATIONS AND EXHIBITIONS*

A. Scholarly Work

"The Chinese Montage: From Poetry and Painting to the Silver Screen," invited contribution in Chris Berry, ed., *Perspectives on Chinese Cinema*, Cornell University East Asian Papers, No. 39, British Film Institute, London, 1991.

Wen Yiduo:Selected Poetry and Prose, translator and editor, Panda Press, Bejing, China, 1990.

"Avalokitesvara (Guanyin) as Savior from Perils," invited contribution by the Getty Center for Education in the Arts, Los Angeles, October 1989.

Chinese Aesthetics and Ch' i Pai-shih, Joint Publishing Co., Hong Kong, 1986.

"Chinese Confluence of Eastern and Western Art," *Asian Culture Quarterly,* Vol. X, No. 2, Summer 1982.

"Chinese Poetry and Painting—Some Observations on Their Interrelationship," *Monumental Serica,* Vol, 34, Germany (1979-80).

"The Beauty of the Nondescriptive in Chinese Painting and Calligraphy," *Journal of The Chinese Language Teachers' Association,* Vol. XIV, No. 1, February 1979.

"Man-Nature Relationship in Chinese Poetry," *Journal of the Chinese Language Teacher's Association,* Vol. XIII, No. 1, February 1978.

B. Creative Work

Drawing of "Wen I-to," *Twentieth Century Literary Criticism,* Vol, 28, Detroit: Dale Research Co, 1988, p. 407.

To Mommy with Love, Taipei, Taiwan, 1988, 2nd ed., 1990, 3rd ed., 1991 (poetry and paintings).

The Many Moods of Catherine Yi-yu Cho Woo. Taipei, Taiwan, 1986 (book of paintings).

Fifteen paintings in *Ming Pao Monthly,* Hong Kong, October 1983.

Dramatic script (in Chinese) based on Chapter Four of Mao Tun's Rainbow (虹).

Eight paintings, six poems in *The Chinese Pen,* Spring 1981, Taipei, Taiwan.

Thousand Yellow Pine, 2nd ed., Art Book Co., Taipei, Taiwan, Fall 1982 (anthology of poetry).

C. Textbooks

The Magic of the Brush, co-authored with Kai-yu Hsu, Art Book Co., Taipei, Taiwan, 1981.

Stroke Order Chart (to be used with John de Francis' *Character Text for Beginning Chinese),* 3rd ed., University Press, SDSU, 1973. (Calligraphy and basic foundation for dictionary usage)

Characters of the Hexagrams of the I Ching, SDSU Press, 1972. (Calligraphy, etymology, and translations)

D. Translations

Poems by Ch'ing Pao-shen, tutor to the last emperor of the Ch'ing Dynasty (Chinese to English). Invited contribution to an anthology of Ch'ing poetry, *Waiting for the Unicorn,* ed. Irving Lo and William Schultz, University of Indiana Press, 1986.

Wen I-to, the Pioneer of Contemporary Chinese Poetry, by Kai-yu Hsu, Po Wen Book Co., Hong Kong, 1982. Serialized in *Chung Pao Monthly,* Hong

Kong, Vols. IV and V, 1980 (English to Chinese).

E. Publications in Chinese

"Spring Rain," *Anthology of Contemporary Chinese Essays,* Vol. II, New Asian Culture Foundations, April 1988.

"Ch'i Pai-shih Belongs to the World," (newspaper article)

Lyrics for songs "First Love" (初恋), "I am Addicted to You" (上了你癮), "Life after Next" (来生　), March 1988.

"Ch'i Pai-shih," *Center Daily News,* New York and Los Angeles, January, 1985.

Music for the Song, "Missing You" (相思已是不曾閑　　), 1986.

"Books," "Waiting," *Center Daily News,* New York and Los Angeles, January 1985 (poems).

"Chinese Poetry, Painting and Culture," *Sino Daily Express,* New York, December 1984.

"Ten Fingers," *United Daily News,* Taipei, Taiwan, and *Chinese Daily News,* San Francisco, September 1983 (poem).

"I Want to Return," "Rain," "Brushes," "Sorrow," *Chinese Daily News,* San Francisco, September 1983 (poems).

"Quietly She Left, as Quietly She Came—Remembering Pai Hsien-ming," *Chinese Daily News,* San Francisco, 1982.

"On Dreams," *Hsin-sheng Daily News,* Taipei, Taiwan, 1982 (article).

Lyrics for the number one popular song in Taiwan, October 1982, "Every Day the Sky a Blue Sapphire" (天天天藍).

F. Exhibitions of Paintings (S # solo: G # group)

Community Memorial Museum, Yuba-Sutter Arts Council, Marysville, California, March, 1992 (S)

Ewing Gallery, University of Tennessee, Knoxville, Tennessee, September, 1991 (S)

California Arts Council Gallery, Sacramento, California, September-December, 1991 (S)

Merced Arts Council, Merced, California, June-July, 1991 (S)

San Diego State University, San Diego, California, February-May, 1991 (S)

Mary Riggs Gallery, La Jolla, California, January, 1990 (S)

Fine Arts Gallery, Kansas City Library, Kansas City, Kansas, November 1-30, 1989 (S)

University of Wyoming, Laramie, Wyoming, August, 1989 (S)

Columbia College, Columbia, Missouri, May-June, 1989 (S)

The American University, Washington, D.C., October-December, 1988 (S)

Hobart and William Smith Colleges, Geneva, New York, January, 1988 (S)

Arthur M. Sackler Museum, Harvard University, October 1-December 31, 1987 (S)

Irvine Fine Arts Center, Irvine, California, September-November, 1987 (S)

Amherst College and the University of Massachusetts, Amherst, Massachusetts, April, 1986 (S)

Tokyo Museum, Tokyo, Japan, December, 1985 (G)

Cork Gallery, Lincoln Center, New York City, August, 1985 (G)

Taipei Fine Arts Museum, August, 1985 (S)

Chinese Culture Center, New York City, November, 1984 (S)

M. Okada Association, "Cultural Olympics," Long Beach, California, June-September, 1984 (S)

Franklin College, Franklin, Indiana, March, 1984 (S)

Seton Hall University, South Orange, New Jersey, February-March, 1984 (S)

National Gallery, National History Museum, Taipei, Taiwan, 1984 (S)

National Hall of Culture and Art Renaissance, Seoul, Korea, December, 1983 (G)

Morehead State University, Morehead, Kentucky, November-December, 1983 (S)

Office of the Chancellor, California State University, Long Beach, California, May-August, 1983 (S)

ART Beasley Gallery, San Diego, California, September-October, 1981 (S)

Wilson Gallery, Fresno, California, March-April, 1982 (S)

ART Beasley Gallery, San Diego, California, October-November, 1981 (S)

Michael Himovitz Gallery, Carmichael, California, October, 1981 (S)

Dragon Gate Gallery, Taipei, Taiwan, July-August, 1981 (S)

Stanford University, Stanford, California, April-July, 1981 (S)

Bank of America, World Headquarters Gallery, San Francisco, California, February-March, 1981 (S)

Office of the Governor, State of California, Sacramento, California, October-November, 1980 (G)

American Culture Center, Taipei, Taiwan, July-August, 1980 (S)

Twenty-four Sather Gallery, Berkeley, California, January-March, 1980 (S)

Paintings on regular display at San Diego Museum of Art, Rental and Sale Gallery, 1977-1981

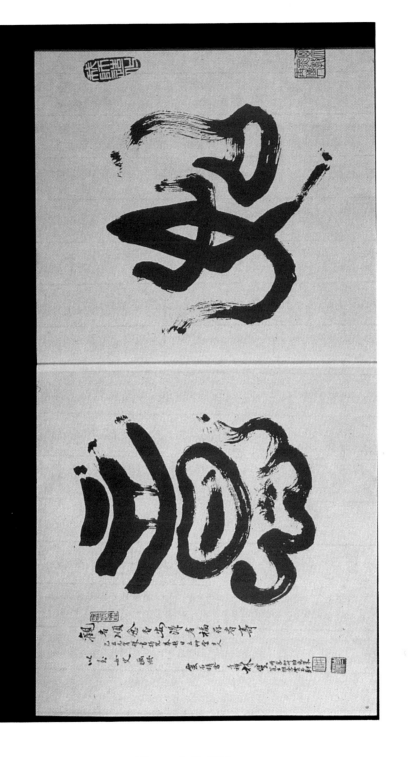

(figure 1: Ju Yi)

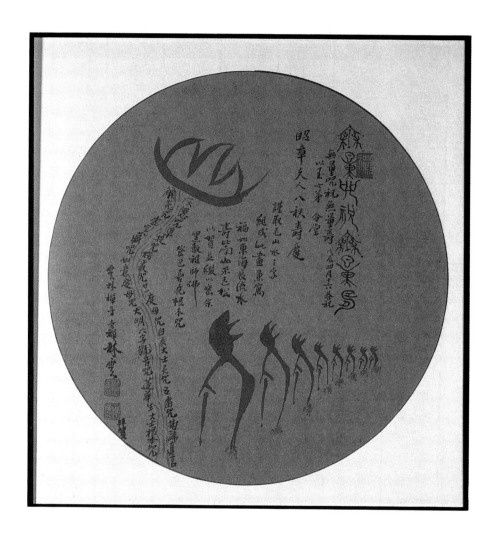

(figure 2: calligraphy painting)

(figure 3: Professor Lin Yun)

(figure 4: Pines)

(figure 5: Misty Peak)

(figure 6: Spring Greetings)

(figure 7: A Patch of Bright Cloud)

(figure 8: Contemplating)

(figure 9: Quiet Roar)

(figure 10: Quiet Roar [close-up])

(figure 11: Immersed in Infinite Joy)

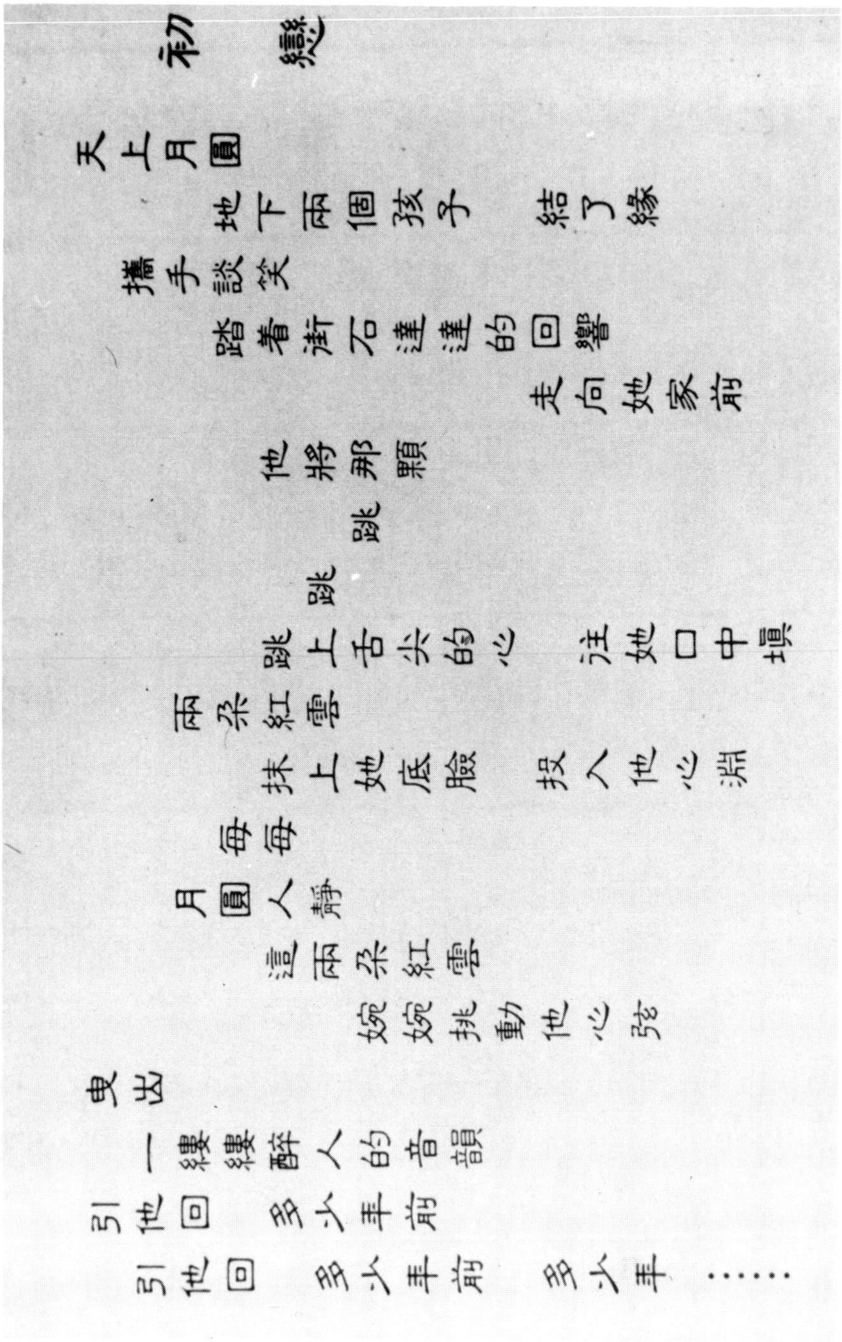

初戀

天上月圓
地下兩個孩子結了緣
攜手談笑
踏着街石達達的回響
走向她家前

他將那顆
跳上跳上舌尖的心
投入她口中
注她心淵

兩朵紅雲跳上她底臉
月圓每每這兩朵紅雲
每人靜靜
婉婉挑動他心弦

曳出
引他回出一縷縷
醉人的音韻
引他回多少年前
多少年前　多少年……

(figure 12: First Love)

(figure 13: Eric Geiger and Odile Reine-Adelaide)

(figure 14: Chance Encounter)

(figure 15: The First Glimpse of Afterglow)

(figure 16: The Seas Frontage)

(figure 17: Contentment)

(figure 18: Softly the Birds Sing)

(figure 19: Kim Chidley and Faith Jensen-Ismay)

(figure 20: Missing You)

(figure 21: Quivering Blue)

(figure 22: Reverberating Joy)

(figure 23: Lush)

(figure 24: Neptune's Heraldry)

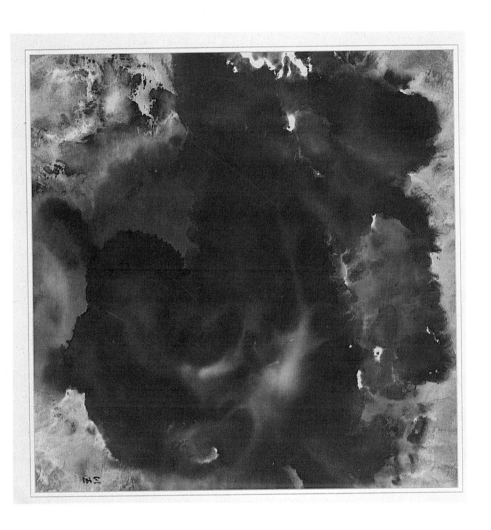

(figure 25: Temptation of Strength)

(figure 26: Bewitched by Spring Dream)

(figure 27: Ch'i)

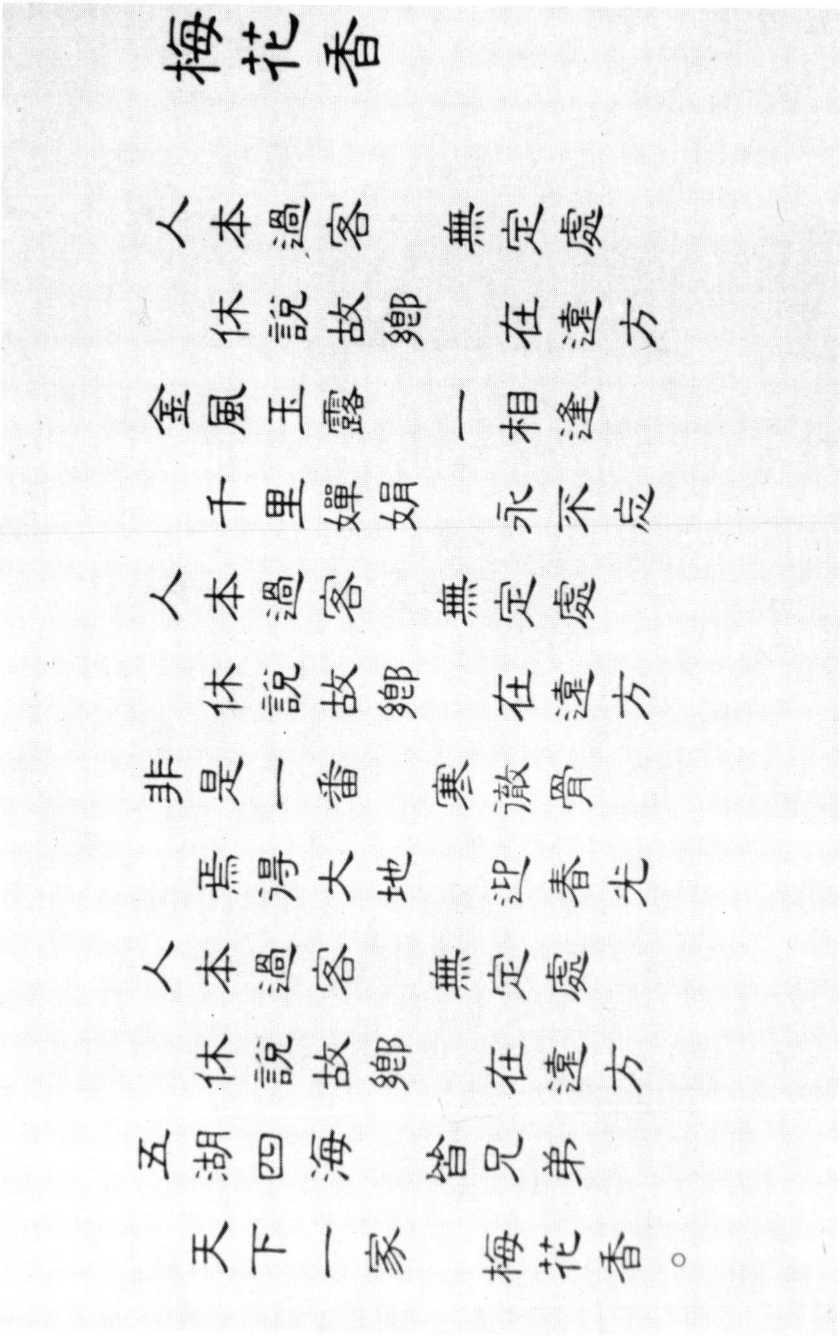

梅花香

人本過客無定處
休說故鄉在遠方
金風玉露一相逢
千里嬋娟永不忘

人本過客無定處
休說故鄉在遠方
非是一番寒徹骨
焉得大地迎春先

人本過客無定處
休說故鄉在遠方
五湖四海皆兄弟
天下一家梅花香。

(figure 28: Plum Blossom Fragrance)

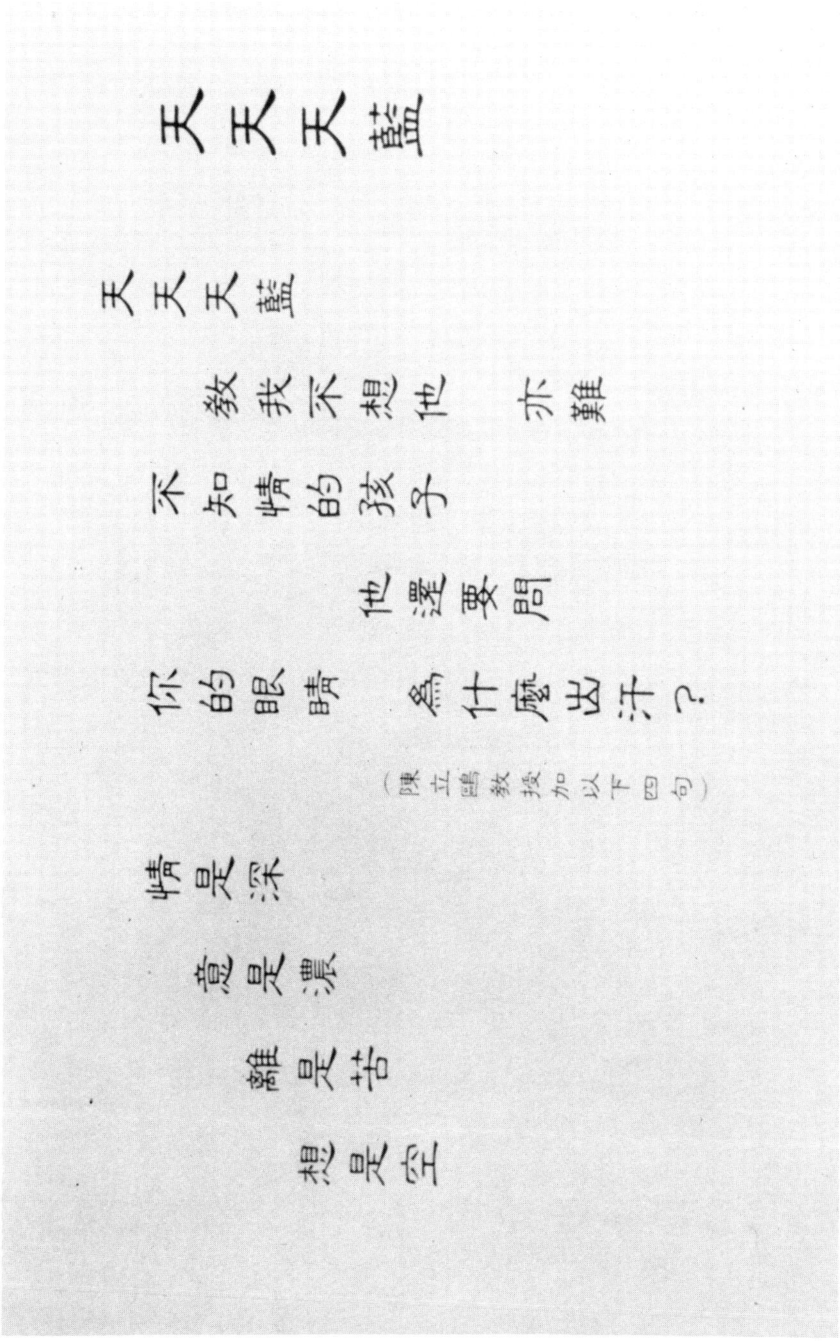

天 天 天 藍

天 天 天 藍

教我不想他
不知情的孩子
他還要問
你的眼睛
為什麼出汗？

亦難

（陳立鷗教授加以下四句）

情是深
意是濃
離是苦
想是空

(figure 29: Tian Tian Tian Lan)

(figure 30: Ch'i Soaring)

(figure 31: William Spencer Noble and Gail Olson)

(figure 32: Professor Zhou Chia-sheng)

(figure 33: Azalea)

(figure 34: Tender Caress)

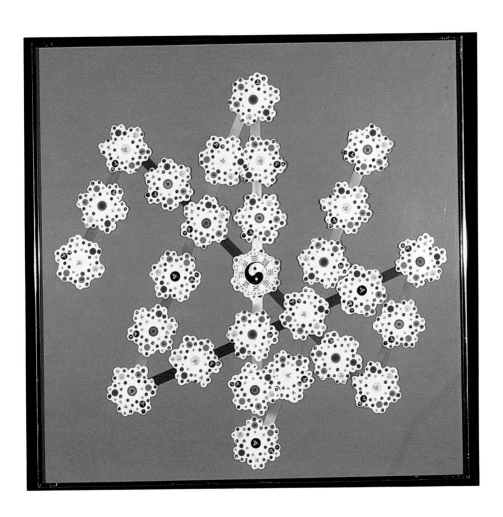

(figure 35: "Nine Stars" Blessing)

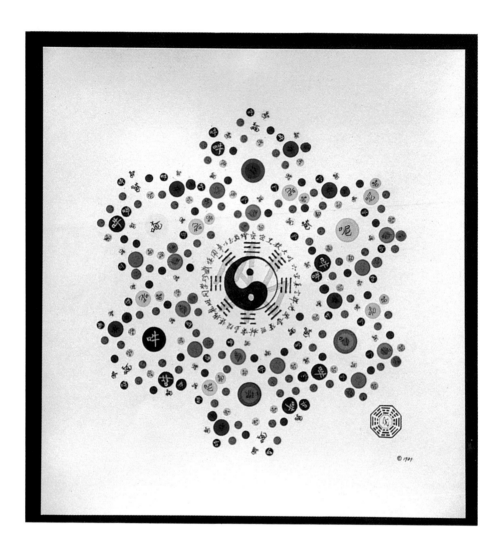

(figure 36: An Ma Ni Ba Mi Hung)